DK READERS

Pre-level 1

Fishy Tales
Colorful Days
Garden Friends
Party Fun
In the Park
Farm Animals
Petting Zoo
Let's Make Music
Meet the Dinosaurs
Duck Pond Dip
My Dress-up Box
On the Move

Snakes Slither and Hiss
Family Vacation
Ponies and Horses
My Day
John Deere: Busy Tractors
LEGO® DUPLO®: On the Farm
Cuentos de Peces *en español*
Dias Ilenos de color *en español*
Star Wars: Blast Off!
Star Wars The Clone Wars: Don't Wake the
  Zillo Beast!

Level 1

A Day at Greenhill Farm
Truck Trouble
Tale of a Tadpole
Surprise Puppy!
Duckling Days
A Day at Seagull Beach
Whatever the Weather
Busy Buzzy Bee
Big Machines
Wild Baby Animals
A Bed for the Winter
Born to be a Butterfly
Dinosaur's Day
Feeding Time
Diving Dolphin
Rockets and Spaceships
My Cat's Secret
First Day at Gymnastics
A Trip to the Zoo
I Can Swim!
A Trip to the Library
A Trip to the Doctor
A Trip to the Dentist
I Want to be a Ballerina
Animal Hide and Seek
Submarines and Submersibles
Animals at Home
Let's Play Soccer
Homes Around the World

LEGO® DUPLO®: Around Town
LEGO® City: Trouble at the Bridge
LEGO® City: Secret at Dolphin Bay
LEGO® Pirates: Blackbeard's Treasure
Star Wars: What is a Wookiee?
Star Wars: Ready, Set, Podrace!
Star Wars: Luke Skywalker's Amazing Story
Star Wars: Tatooine Adventures
Star Wars The Clone Wars: Watch Out for
  Jabba the Hutt!
Star Wars The Clone Wars: Pirates... and
  Worse
Power Rangers: Jungle Fury: We are the
  Power Rangers
Indiana Jones: Indy's Adventures
John Deere: Good Morning, Farm!
A Day in the Life of a Builder
A Day in the Life of a Dancer
A Day in the Life of a Firefighter
A Day in the Life of a Teacher
A Day in the Life of a Musician
A Day in the Life of a Doctor
A Day in the Life of a Police Officer
A Day in the Life of a TV Reporter
Gigantes de Hierro *en español*
Crías del mundo animal *en español*

A Note to Parents

DK READERS is a compelling program for beginning readers, designed in conjunction with leading literacy experts, including Dr. Linda Gambrell, Distinguished Professor of Education at Clemson University. Dr. Gambrell has served as President of the National Reading Conference, the College Reading Association, and the International Reading Association.

Beautiful illustrations and superb full-color photographs combine with engaging, easy-to-read stories to offer a fresh approach to each subject in the series. Each DK READER is guaranteed to capture a child's interest while developing his or her reading skills, general knowledge, and love of reading.

The five levels of DK READERS are aimed at different reading abilities, enabling you to choose the books that are exactly right for your child:

Pre-level 1: Learning to read
Level 1: Beginning to read
Level 2: Beginning to read alone
Level 3: Reading alone
Level 4: Proficient readers

The "normal" age at which a child begins to read can be anywhere from three to eight years old. Adult participation through the lower levels is very helpful for providing encouragement, discussing storylines, and sounding out unfamiliar words.

No matter which level you select, you can be sure that you are helping your child learn to read, then read to learn!

DK

LONDON, NEW YORK, MUNICH,
MELBOURNE, AND DELHI

Series Editor Deborah Lock
U.S. Editor Shannon Beatty
Designer Rosie Levine
Production Editor Sean Daly
Picture Researcher Rob Nunn
Jacket Designer Natalie Godwin

Reading Consultant
Linda Gambrell, Ph.D

First American Edition, 2011
Published in the United States by
DK Publishing
375 Hudson Street, New York, New York 10014

11 12 13 14 15 10 9 8 7 6 5 4 3 2 1
001-182472-August 2011

Published in Great Britain by Dorling Kindersley Limited.

A catalog record for this book is available
from the Library of Congress.

ISBN: 978-0-7566-8930-8 (paperback)
ISBN: 978-0-7566-8931-5 (hardcover)

DK books are available at special discounts when purchased in bulk
for sales promotions, premiums, fund-raising, or educational use.
For details, contact:
DK Publishing Special Markets
375 Hudson Street
New York, New York 10014
SpecialSales@dk.com

Printed and bound in China by L Rex Printing Co., Ltd.

The publisher would like to thank the following for their kind
permission to reproduce their photographs:
a=above, b=below/bottom, c=center, l=left, r=right, t=top

Alamy Images: D. Hurst 18fbr; Nikreates 19bc, 31br; Pegaz 20-21.
Corbis: Heide Benser 26-27; Randy Faris 4; Move Art Management
5. **Getty Images:** Fuse 10t; The Image Bank / John Kelly 19t; The
Image Bank / Martin Poole 16t; Lifesize / Yellow Dog Productions
18c, 32clb; Stockbyte / Steve Wisbauer 18br.

All other images © Dorling Kindersley
For further information see www.dkimages.com

Discover more at
www.dk.com

Contents

DK READERS

LEARNING
pre-level
1
TO READ

My Day

DK
DK Publishing

Good morning!
I wake up and stretch.

arm

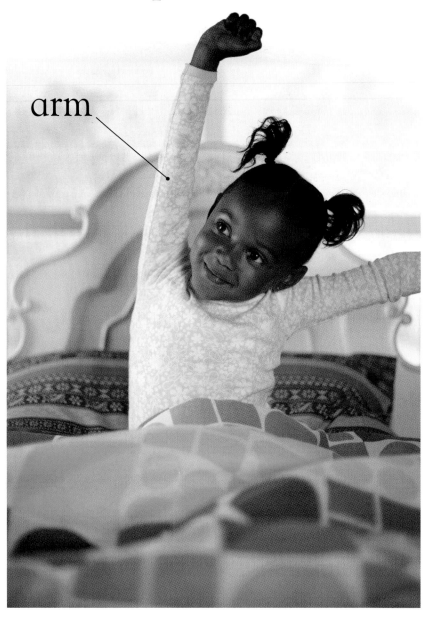

It's the start
of a new day.

I wash my face
and put on
my clothes.

T-shirt

 clothes

hanger

 breakfast

I sit down to eat my breakfast.

cereal

bowl

shoelaces

shoes

I put on my shoes
and my coat
for school.

coat

I play with
the shapes at school.

 shapes

square

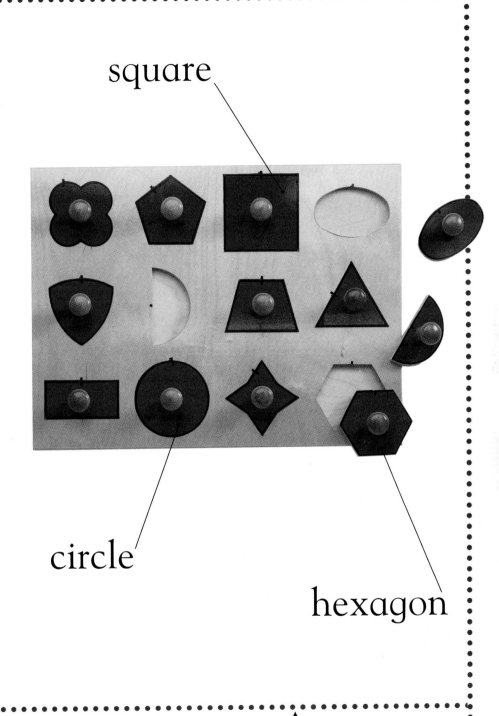

circle

hexagon

 games

I learn games with my class.

It's lunchtime!

apple

water

I sit down
to eat my lunch.

 lunch

tricycle

playground

I ride and swing and
slide at the playground.

Good afternoon!

 music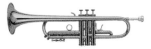

I jump around to music
before I go home.

I play with my toys
when I get home.

train

doll

ball

 toys

peas

 cook

24

rice

I help
cook dinner.

I take a bath and brush
my teeth after eating
my dinner.

bathrobe

bathtime

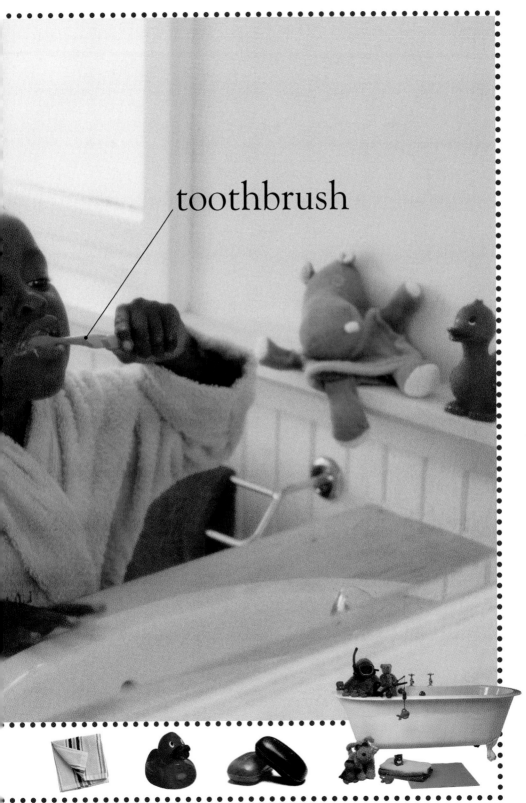

toothbrush

book

pajamas

I put on my pajamas
and then read a book.

teddy bear

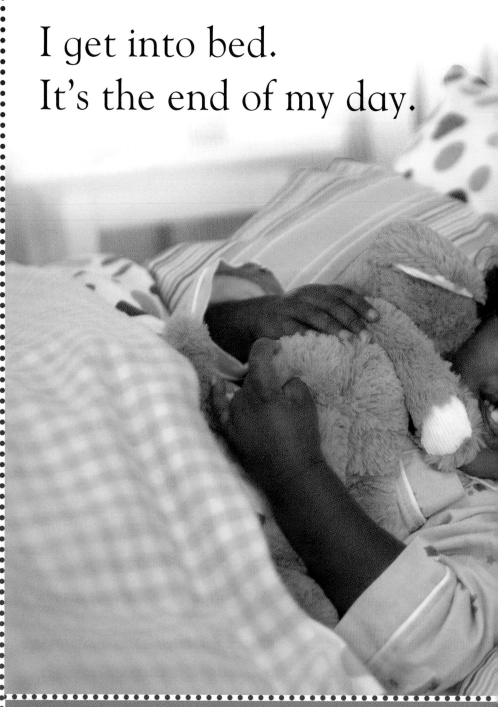

I get into bed.
It's the end of my day.

 What did you like

Goodnight!

doing today?

Glossary

Breakfast
is the first meal
of the day.

Cook
is to make food
ready for eating.

Lunch
is a meal eaten in
the middle of the day.

Playground
is an outdoor place
where children play.

School
is a building where
children go to learn.

Index